THE CHANGIN

Cumnor and Farmoor
with Appleton and Eaton

Norman Dix
and
John Hanson

for Cumnor History Society

Published by
Robert Boyd Publications
260 Colwell Drive
Witney, Oxfordshire OX8 7LW

First published 1996

ISBN 1 899536 11 6

OTHER TITLES IN THE
CHANGING FACES SERIES
Cowley
Cowley: Book Two
Summertown and Cutteslowe
Botley and North Hinksey
Headington: Book One
Littlemore and Sandford
Woodstock
Marston: Book One
Cumnor and Farmoor with Appleton and Eaton

Printed and bound in Great Britain at The Alden Press, Oxford

Contents

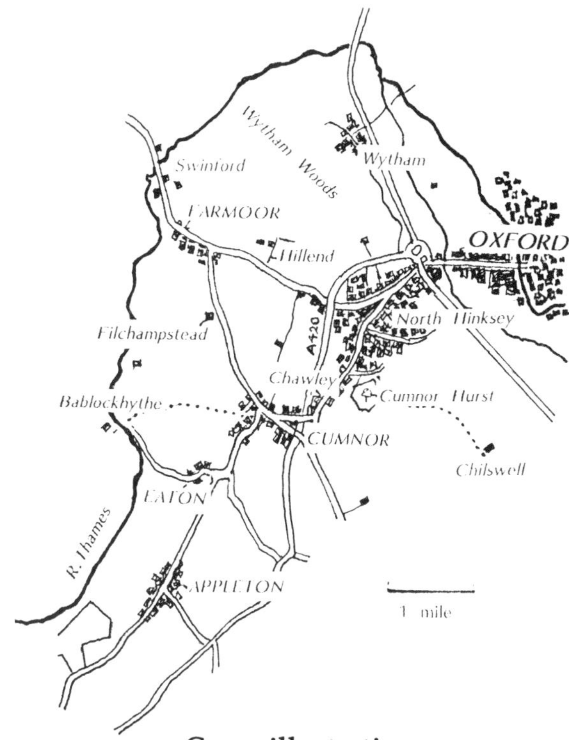

Cover illustrations

Front: 'Dad Charlie' Costar of Cumnor
(Photograph 1960: Oxford and County Newspapers)

Back: Appleton blacksmiths

We must begin on a sad note – that Ted Drury, who was to help in compiling this book, died shortly before work began on it. He took an active interest in many aspects of parish life, and his passing denied us his rich experience. Through the kindness of Marjorie, Ted's album of parish photographs has been taken into the History Society's archives.

Ted Drury

Acknowledgements

Many photographs have been available to us from the extensive archive of Cumnor History Society. We have also been able to draw on the albums compiled by Mike Baston at Farmoor, Mrs J. Edmonds and Philip Powell in Cumnor, and John Cox. Their considerable help we gladly acknowledge. We express particular gratitude for help given by Christopher Cowley and staff at Oxford & County Newspapers and by Malcolm Graham and staff at the Centre for Oxfordshire Studies. We are also indebted to the following for their help: Jim and Heather Adams, Harold Clack, Mrs M. Crapper, Dennis Eden, David Farrant, Mrs Janet Gow, Francis Harris, Mrs Mary Hayward, Mrs Elizabeth Hawtin, Stewart Simmonds, Dick Smith, Cedric Tyrrell, Eric and Iris Wastie, Frank Webb, Ralph and Frank White. We acknowledge with thanks the consent given to use pictures by Thames Water plc. and Charlotte James, publishers. We would also thank those original owners of photographs whom we were unable to trace. (Where a name is acknowledged below a photograph, it indicates the owner and/or the photographer.)

Preface

Cumnor and Appleton are neighbouring parishes but historically they lay in different Hundreds of Berkshire and were owned by different lords of the manor. There were, however, always strong social ties between the two communities and many a marriage partner was found by exploring over the shared parish boundary. People often moved from one parish to the other in search of better prospects, the grass appearing greener on the other side. Less than century ago, elderly Cumnor residents would playfully refer to visitors from Appleton as 'they forriners', but, while the area in Victorian times did have a sense of isolation, few families in either parish were without relatives in the other, so strong was the web of kinship in those rural communities. Our aim has been to recapture the more rural character of Cumnor and Appleton in former days and to illustrate the changes that have occured since.

(Photo: Eden)

Cumnor village High Street in 1912 (photo: Taunt)

SECTION ONE

Cumnor: an Introduction

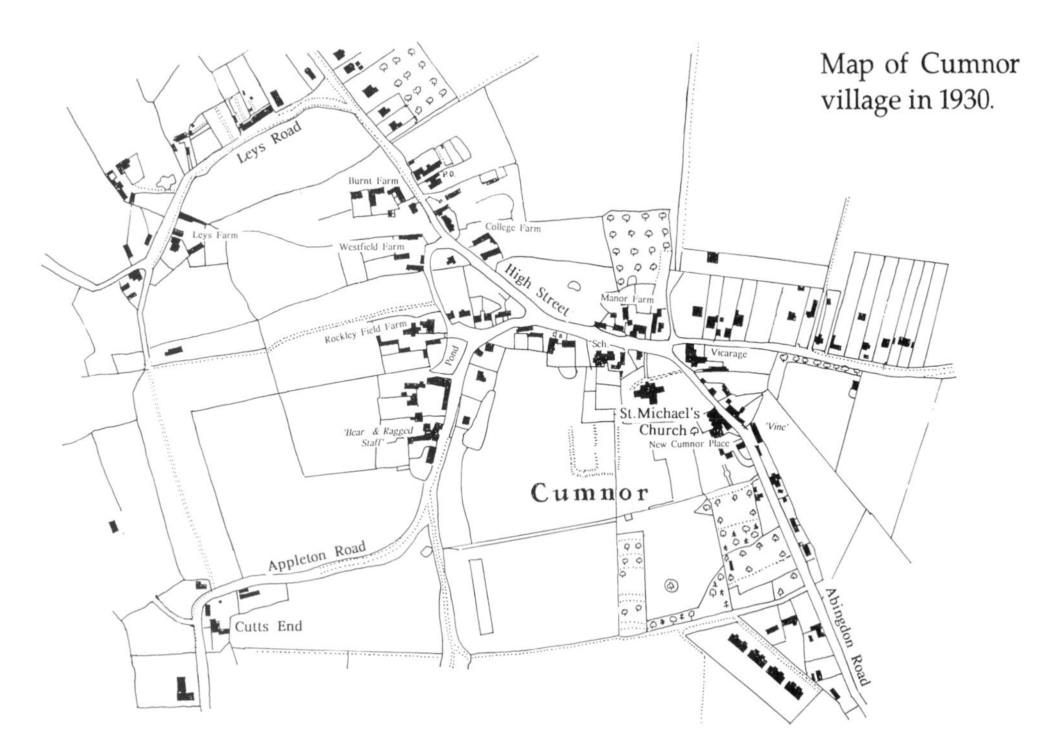

Map of Cumnor village in 1930.

Aerial view of the village from the south-west. (Photo: Dick Smith)

Cumnor village lies at the centre of a large parish which in medieval times was one of the richest possessions of Abingdon Abbey. After the Dissolution it passed through several hands before being acquired, through marriage, by the Bertie family. James Bertie was created Earl of Abingdon in 1682 and his successors held the manor and its lands until financial problems forced the 8th Earl to sell his estates in the 1920s.

In Victorian times the village was much visited on account of the stories surrounding the mysterious death of Amy, wife of Robert Dudley, later Earl of Leicester, at Cumnor Place in 1560, an interest kindled by Scott's popular novel 'Kenilworth'. The remains of Cumnor Place, however, had been pulled down in 1811.

Cumnor Place, drawn a few years before the ruins were demolished 1809–1812.

Here was countryside enjoyed by Matthew Arnold, who knew well the 'warm green-muffled Cumnor hills', Bablockhythe on the Thames, Chilswell, and Cumnor Hurst, where one looked down on Oxford's 'dreaming spires'.

Cumnor Hurst, photographed by Taunt 100 years ago. In medieval times the hillside was the manorial warren (enclosure for rabbits, hares and partridges).

Chilswell Farm c.1900 (photo: Taunt)

Bablockhythe ferry in 1859 (woodcut: Hall). Though often associated with Cumnor, the ferry and its alehouse lay within the boundaries of Northmoor parish.

By 1900 a recession in agriculture, on which the local economy depended, had brought an air of neglect to the parish. Cumnor village, guidebooks advised, was 'emphatically not residential'. Since 1921 the population of the parish, with its former hamlets at Farmoor, Chawley and Dean Court, has risen four-fold and it has become a highly desirable residential area. For centuries dependent almost entirely on its rural economy, much of the parish is now a dormitory for Oxford.

SECTION TWO

St. Michael's Parish Church

Dr Vyse's drawing in 1774 showed the church and the remains of Cumnor Place still standing to the west.

Wood's watercolour in 1890 was painted from across the road. The rear of Church Cottage is visible but the cottage seen behind it no longer exists.

This interior view of the church, with its oil lamps and stove, was taken early in the century.

The parish church of St. Michael's at Cumnor was always considered by visitors to be among the finest in the district. Of Saxon origin, its mainly medieval structure has survived relatively unscathed through the centuries and still occupies a central place in the community.

Grigg's sketch of the church in 1906, drawn from the churchyard, included the chest tomb of Lt. William Godfrey of Chawley.

The Rev. Samuel Griffith was vicar from 1877 to 1903 and took a close interest in parish affairs.

A statue of Queen Elizabeth, sketched by A. Forrester in 1846 at a farm near North Hinksey, was later brought to the church vestry by the Rev. S. Griffith.

At 11.00 a.m. on Sunday 3rd September 1939, the Rev. Dudley Buston began Matins in the church as Neville Chamberlain broadcast his declaration of war. At the service, Banns of Marriage were read out for William Buckingham of Cumnor and Edith Stimpson of Appleton.

SECTION THREE

Abingdon Road

View of Cumnor Vicarage c.1920. It was first mentioned in 1298, though the present building dates from many later periods. In 1728, less sober times, the inventory of the Rev. William Peacock included 'ye Brewhouse', 'ye Ale cellar', and 'ye Small beer Buttery'.

Rev. Henry Hall, vicar 1930–1938, had previously taught for 35 years in an Oxford school.

Rev. D.G.Buston, vicar 1939–1950.

New Cumnor Place from the Abingdon road c.1912 (Taunt).

The west front of New Cumnor Place c.1920.

New Cumnor Place probably dates from the end of the 16th century, though many additions and changes have been made since. Lord Abingdon's first attempt to sell the freehold in 1892 (when the tenant was Mrs Weaving, widow of a brewer) ended in the Chancery Court after the purchaser at auction, a Rev. E. Scott-Hall, refused to pay. He claimed that the estate agent had misled him into believing it was the house where Amy Dudley died!

Mr and Mrs Loat, who acquired the New Cumnor Place at the turn of the century, prepare for an outing. The coachman was James Webb, who also worked as their gardener.

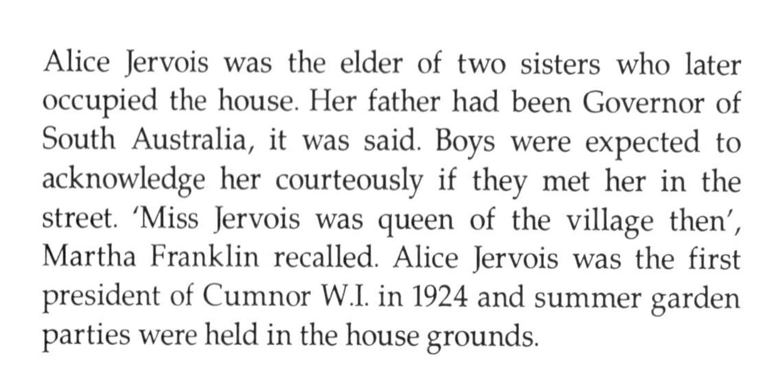

Alice Jervois was the elder of two sisters who later occupied the house. Her father had been Governor of South Australia, it was said. Boys were expected to acknowledge her courteously if they met her in the street. 'Miss Jervois was queen of the village then', Martha Franklin recalled. Alice Jervois was the first president of Cumnor W.I. in 1924 and summer garden parties were held in the house grounds.

The 'Vine' was built in 1743 but did not become a public house till the end of the last century. It took its name from the old alehouse that had stood in the High Street. The first landlord was Thyoth Godfrey, a blacksmith, and his brick-built workshop stood by the road.

Cottage (now No. 19) in 1940. It was one of the early cottages built 'on the waste', the wide verge of the old road. When it was sold by the executors of Miss Alice Jervois in 1950 it comprised one bedroom and a landing room, a living room and a bucket closet, the rent being 4s 6d a week.

Cottages (Nos. 5, 7 and 9) in 1940. The three cottages were sold for £645 in 1950. The tenants were Mrs Didcock, Mr Sallis, and, at No. 9, Mr Bowden.

Looking northward down the Abingdon road c.1920.

SECTION FOUR

Oxford Road

Oxford Road, looking east c.1960. Cumnor Hurst can be seen in the distance.

Amy Hick's grocery store in the 1930s. Her brother ran a garage business at the back, which also served petrol.

Historically you had arrived at Cumnor when you came down Bowling Alley Road (now Oxford Road) and reached the vicarage. The authors of *Wanderings with a Pen and Pencil* in 1846 wrote: 'You enter the village of Cumnor from a deep and narrow road with a footpath to the right of the causeway, a lengthened wall upon your left defending the gardens in the rearward of the rectory, a similar stone fence opposite forming a mossy boundary to pleasant orchards terraced by nature above the main road.'

SECTION FIVE

Cumnor School

Cumnor School opened in 1860 and for almost a hundred years provided an elementary education for parish children. Until transport was provided in 1926, some children had to walk three miles to school.

The school c.1931. The car is said to have belonged to a visiting music teacher.

Offences resulting in 'three stripes with cane' in 1930: 'Snowballing Assistant Mistress on way to school'; 'chattering in lessons'; 'rebellious'; 'complete indifference to teacher's suggestions'; 'speaking in Drill lesson'; 'left seat without permission'.

The infants' class of 1924. At the front, 4th from left: Frank Webb. Can anyone identify the following children who were admitted to school that same year? Basil Grimes from Upper Whitley, Reginald Cox of Farmoor, William Belcher, Albert Lardner of Lower Whitley, Cynthia Chilvers of Oaken Holt Lodge, Anthony Broadis of Farmoor Lane cottage, Kenneth Bateman.

A class of 1935. Back row, left to right: Phyllis Didcock, Peggy Edwards, Sylvia Costar, Marjorie Benstead, Eva Hutt, Molly Hansen. Middle row: Marjory Rackcliffe, Hazel Bateman, Roland Hutt, Henry Hathaway, Derek Sparks, Ronald Webb, James Neale, Nesbit Broadis, Rosina Willoughby, Georgina Howe. Sitting: Betty Towill, Helene Astell, Mary Hirons, Betty Hansen, Glenys Russell.

The headteacher's log book showed that in September 1939 the school was under great strain: 129 children, evacuated from Silverton in London's East End were taught in the afternoon, while another 55 from Bow were taught in the village hall.

School group in 1951, outside village hall. Back row, left to right: Richard Dabney, –, Gillian Webb, Brian Buckingham, –, –, Peter Bruton, Geoff Adfield. Middle row: John Carter, Mike Jennings, Edward Ayton, Peter Clack, Pat Savage, –, –, –, –, Stephen Stockford, Keith Hickman, Dennis Eden, Terry Rogers. Front row: –, Anne Floyd, –, –, –, Ruth Alexander, –.

The old school building could not meet the needs of the growing parish population after the war. In 1952 a new primary school was built off Oxford Road.

The old school building was used for village meetings but fell into disrepair. In 1995, under new Trustees, an improvement scheme for the 'Old School' was launched. The school house was adapted to accommodate a police office and a new location for the village Post Office and greengrocer's. The photo shows the opening of the new shops in 1995.

Chris Durrant.
His energetic management did so much to bring a new look to the old buildings.

SECTION SIX

Cumnor High Street

The old 'Vine', haven for thirsty bell-ringers, was built in the 16th century as a cottage and stood on the corner of the main street and Gurney's (now Gee's) Lane until about 1850, when it was pulled down. After Scott's *Kenilworth* was published, the alehouse was renamed the 'Jolly Black Bear' to catch the tourist trade. This drawing, of unknown date, is said to have been given to Monty Sherwood on his wedding by the Rev.H. Hall.

In 1900 a brick house was built on the site by Frewin. This photograph was taken c.1910. (Taunt)

Looking down the High Street in 1912. The farmhouse on the right, soon to be named 'Manor Farm', was for centuries known as 'Ruffins'. It stood next to the old 'Vine'. Opposite the farm was 'Church Cottage', where a well provided water for the cottagers and the churchyard.

Looking down the High Street in 1996.

Church House in 1912. It dates from the early 16th century, when it was used for brewing 'church ales'. It was later an alms house.

Mrs Harvey's mother, Mrs Matthews, at the second door of Church House some 70 years ago, with Mrs Harvey's son.

Mr Harvey with his mother-in-law Mrs Matthews and her son Mr Money, at the street gate to Church House.

Looking up the High Street c.1910. The barn on the left was redeveloped for residential use a few years ago.

The view in 1990.

The Women's Branch of the British Legion in procession to St.Michael's Church for the dedication of their Colours in 1950. The tythe barn is to the left. The old cottages, Nos. 9–13, can be seen in the background.

The old cottages at 9–13 High Street. They were demolished in 1963.

This view shows part of the High Street in 1960. Westfield Farm house stands in the background. North of it was a yard where Harold Clack kept his coaches; he lived across the road.

Harry Willoughby outside his cottage in the terrace that lay at right-angles to the High Street. He lost a leg in an accident at Chawley Works and bought his cottage with the £70 compensation. In 1921 the occupants of two adjoining cottages had suffered misfortune when they joined a strike at Chawley: Lord Abingdon's agent brought in bailiffs to eject them, leaving the families and their furniture in the street.

Emma Clack (née Sherwood) outside her High Street cottage, which was pulled down in 1965. She married Joseph Clack who was born in Northmoor.

'Burnt Farm' in 1976. The building dates back to the late 17th century, though a farm was recorded here long before. Harry and Hilda Webb lived here during and after the Second World War. The name was borrowed from an adjoining farm which burnt down in 1784 and was never rebuilt. Hilda said that the 'knot garden' at the front was created by Harry's great-grandfather.

A bird's-eye view of the former greengrocer's and the Post Office where from 1927 Joseph Wing, and more recently Jim and Heather Adams, provided many years service. The Post Office had previously been at Hale's in the Oxford Road.

The buildings that had occupied the site (now No. 44). In the 18th century they were occupied by Richard Stephens, blacksmith.

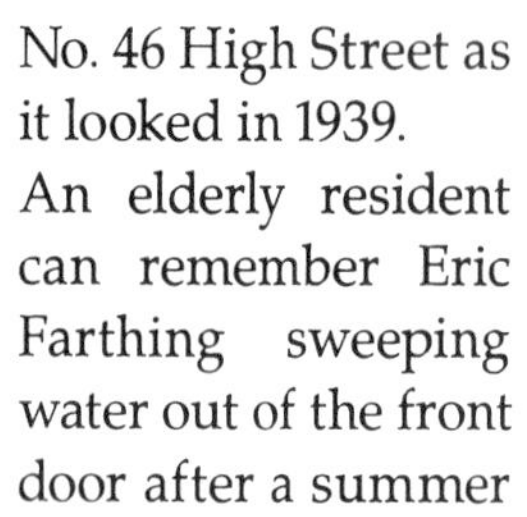

No. 46 High Street as it looked in 1939.
An elderly resident can remember Eric Farthing sweeping water out of the front door after a summer storm and singing 'A Life on the Ocean Waves'. A later tenant, 'Minky' Sherwood, would kill and cure 'cottage pigs'. The several small dwellings in a block to the rear included that of Bessie Pike, who kept a sweet shop in her parlour.

SECTION SEVEN

Leys Road

The 'Lion' elm tree at the junction of Leys Road was a well-known feature. It was a favourite meeting place for a chat and Mrs F. Masters recalled it was the Thursday stopping place for the horse-drawn van and agent, Mr Slay, who brought material and took away the garments, mainly trousers, that village women made up. They were paid 3½d a garment. The 'Lion Tree' was so called because the 'Red Lion', a public house, had for many years occupied the corner site where the village hall was built in 1927.

This view across to Leys Road dates from 1912. It shows again the 'Lion Tree', and also the chapel built in 1895. Non-conformists had previously been meeting, since 1850, in a farm out-building at the bottom of Leys Road.

This cottage was first recorded in 1613. A second storey was added around 1850. It was held for three centuries by Poor Trustees, who took rent from the tenants and spent it on relieving the poor inhabitants of the village. Formerly the two halves had four acres each of farming land. Photo: 1940

These cottages, Nos. 38 and 40, were once part of a farm on this site, held in 1524 by John Bechye.

A wall tablet on this cottage gives the date 1727 and the initials of Bartholomew Innes. In 1871 it was a farmstead with 87 acres but by 1900 it was described as a smallholding held by John Sherwood, a mason. His son 'Monty' was for many years chairman of the Parish Council, a village cricketer and a popular member of the community. (Photo: Wheat 1952)

Leys Farm is one of the few old village farms that remains a working farm today. It was purchased from Lord Abingdon in 1925 by Arthur Wastie but times were hard, owing to the farming recession, and he had to sell some of the land. Arthur Wastie is remembered as an exceptional marksman, being able to 'hit a silver 3d piece in the air or mark his initials on a target board'. Selling hundreds of rabbits he shot on the farm for a shilling each helped to make ends meet.

Neighbours, from left to right: 'Monty' Sherwood, boy, Charlie Costar and Arthur Wastie. c.1932.

Pond Farm burnt down in 1974. It was held for almost 100 years by the Buckingham family. George Buckingham, who lived here in the early years of this century, was listed as a coal and wood dealer but also kept a small herd of cows. His son Albert was a dairyman.

At a cottage, now gone, where his father John ran a market garden, Charles ('Dad Charlie') Costar poses with his wife Louisa and young family, c.1910. He was the last local man to obtain a first job at an Abingdon Hiring Fair.

'Closes' cottage dates in part from the 16th century. This photograph was taken in 1940. Richard Stone, farmer, held it as a freehold in the 18th century. In Victorian times it became home to two families of farm labourers. (Photo: Arkell)

'Dad Charlie' Costar (seated) with wife and relatives, making hay in the grounds of Closes Cottage. He was a gardener, handyman and well-digger.

SECTION EIGHT

Appleton Road

A view in 1914 towards Appleton Road from the High Street. This spot was known as 'Workhouse Corner' and was a favourite meeting place for young men of the village. The thatched houses on the right were formerly 'Willis's Farm' but in the last century became homes for farmworkers. The last beaten-earth floor was replaced only in the 1930s, when main water and electricity supplies reached the main streets in the village. At that time Jemima Saunders kept a small shop at the near end of the former farmhouse.

Looking across the village pond, which according to local folklore never froze after Amy Dudley's ghost was laid to rest there. The cottage on the right became the village poor house in 1800 but by 1861 George Howse was running a first Post Office there. Some people today remember it as the home of Edmund Holifield, plumber. The photo was taken in 1914.

Rockley Field Farm 60 years ago, when Percy Walker farmed there. 'I remember going scrumping in his orchard', one elderly villager recalls. 'His apples always seemed to taste better than ours!'

This cottage, now No.12, dates from the 16th century. Between the wars Frank Didcock ran a coal-delivery business from here, though he had one 'hook arm'. Pat Fowler kept a grocery shop in the front room. 'I used to go round to Didcock's', one villager recollects. 'You'd ask for five Woodbines and she'd wrap them up in a piece of newspaper. Nothing was too much trouble '

The 'Bear and Ragged Staff' was originally built in Elizabethan times as a gentleman's 'cottage'. It was owned by St John's College as Lord of Eaton manor. It only became a public house in about 1860, when the old alehouse in the High Street was pulled down. Photo c.1900.

A row of five cottages stood next to the 'Bear and Ragged Staff'. This photo was taken before the building was abandoned for residential use in the 1950s. Among the last tenants were Mrs Trinder, Mrs G Drewett, Mrs Heavens and William Cox.

SECTION NINE

Cutts End

Cutts End was a satellite of Cumnor, though one of its farms lay within Eaton Parish.

Cutts End Farm was established in 1630. From 1814 till the Second World War it was a small dairy farm run by the Clandfield family. After the war the house was the home of Hubert and Barbara Curtis. Photo 1940.

Hubert Curtis.

Leslie Brooke, who built 'Hurstcote', was a writer and illustrator of children's books. He established a fine garden, which was tended by Arthur Boyles. His son Henry entered politics and became Home Secretary in the 1950s.

Cutts End House was designed by Clough Williams-Ellis in 1911 for Miss Lily Dougal, who lived there for almost 30 years. She was a writer of theological books.

This house, adjoining Cutts End House, was a farm within Eaton. It was called 'Cutts' in John Franklin's will of 1583 and remained a farmstead until the early years of this century. Photo c.1940.

The Appleton road, leading into Cutts End, in 1950. The former 'Cutts' farmhouse is on the left.

Mrs Enoch talking with the elderly Mrs Wickson at the gate of No. 30 in 1928.

The cottage for sale in 1976 (photo: Philip Powell). Since 1935 it was known as 'Moss's' and Percy Moss ran a garage at the side for many years.

The same cottage in 1990.

SECTION TEN

Chawley

Chawley was a tything and hamlet apart from Cumnor village and was separated from it by open fields until within living memory.

'Hillside' at the bottom of Chawley Lane was the farmstead of William Godfrey, who fought as a Cavalier officer at Edgehill and later Civil War battles. His chest tomb can be seen in St. Michael's churchyard.

This farmhouse in Chawley Lane, dating from the late 16th century and known now as 'Bornholm', was derelict in 1991 but plans have been submitted for site redevelopment.

'Chawley Farm' was held by the Peacock family in the 17th century. Henry Tyrrell acquired it at the beginning of this century.

'Blind Pinnock's' cottage was last occupied by Charles Alder. It was demolished in 1935. In the 17th century it had been a popular alehouse.

A view across the valley from Chawley hillside in the first years of this century. Today the A420 by-pass runs across the foreground.

'Rocklands' (now No. 112), one of the first 'villas' to be built on Cumnor Hill.

A view from the top of the clay workings at Chawley, looking NW past the work's chimney to Wytham Hill, c.1910.

Chawley Brick and Tile Works was established around 1845 by John Neale, who occupied the farm across the road (thereafter known as Brick Kiln Farm). By the 1930s its output could not compete with the mass production methods of large, more modern works. Land that was sold off became the development site of Bertie and Norreys Road, where building was interrupted by the Second World War. The works closed in 1939 and part of the site was acquired by Kempfer, a Jewish refugee from Hungary, to start a timber company. The rest of the site was acquired in 1954.

Part of Chawley Works, near the end of its days.

Two workmen with a steam traction engine used to transport heavy timber.

SECTION ELEVEN

Farming

In later Victorian times, Free Trade resulted in a decline in farming. Farmers, without support, were unable to compete with cheap foreign imports of meat and cereals. Lacking investment, Cumnor too fell into decline. Lord Abingdon, the chief landowner, faced growing financial problems and, in the 1920s, sold his estates. It was the Second World War that put agriculture back on a firm, strong footing.

H. Tyrrell at his shop in Oxford Market in the early years of the century. Market-gardening and market outlets were two of the means by which farmers sought to overcome the recession.

John Floyd cutting the meadow hay at Swinford Farm c.1920.

William Eden leading the horse-team as the crop was brought from the 'Clays' on Denman's Farm some 60 years ago.

Working on Mr. Beaumont's Valley Farm at Farmoor in 1943. Left to right: Ernest Barnett, John Clack, George and Paul, and Ernest J. Webb (who later bought the farm). 'George' and 'Paul' were two German prisoners of war. Many farms acquired extra labour in this way.

Cyril Buckingham rolling the 'Clays' in 1960. In the valley, below left, the meadows await the first reservoir.

Frank Webb in 1960 with his champion Guernsey cow, Farmoor Joyce, at Valley Farm. Much of his farmland was taken for the reservoirs.

Drawing of Denmans Farm, looking towards Wytham Hill, in 1976. Elms still punctuated the valley then but a few years later were all lost to Dutch Elm disease.

SECTION TWELVE

Village Life in Cumnor

A blacksmith's workshop in Cumnor in 1890. The worker on the right is said to be Peter Minns from Wootton. There were two blacksmiths in the village at that time but this smithy is likely to be the new building outside the 'Vine'. A craftsman at work was a familiar sight in rural villages.

Waiting for the horse carriages and waggons to arrive. Swinford toll bridge c.1900. Mr Harris, the Eynsham carrier, would make market day trips along the Eynsham road to Oxford, picking up business and passengers along the way.

Joe Clack. 'He could walk the legs off anybody.'

Jimmy Bennett married Gertrude Cox.

Aubrey Trinder married Alice Jackson in 1909. This photo was taken at St. Giles Fair. He became a gamekeeper at Long Leys.

Mrs Costar, wife of 'Big Charlie' Costar, the carter, and their son George. They lived in one of the cottages, the 'Court', near the tythe barn.

Richard Castle was in the Veterinary Corps in the First World War. 'He breathed and lived horses'. He was pictured here with his family. Left to right, back: daughter Ida, who married a Mr Holton of Wendlebury, Lillian, who married George Bateman, Miriam, who married George Harris of Eynsham and settled in Farmoor. Front: Betty, who wed a Mr Bishop of North Hinksey, and Sarah, Richard's first wife.

The Brown brothers, who formed a hand-bell ringing team in Cumnor in the 1920s. Clockwise from back left: Fred, Ted, Gerald, Bert, Bill and Dick.

The cricket XI of 1927 which won the Eynsham Cup. Left to right, back: Charles Hoborough, Arthur Boyles, Henry Brooke, Dick Walker, Frank Bennett. Middle: Cyril Boyles, Henry Hickman, Denton Brown (capt.), Jack Walker, Percy Costar. Sitting: Dick Bennett, Ted Pratley. Cricket was first played in Cumnor in the 1860s.

The Ladies Cricket Team of 1922. Left to right, back: C. Cole, M. Walker, M. Hale, F. Bennett, H. Neale. Front: H. Jeffs, M. Frewin, B. Lambourne, H. Woodward, D. Woodward.

Between the wars women began to take a much more active part in village life.

Mrs Mary Cox on her husband Sydney's motorbike c.1928. (Photo: Cox)

Outside what was later 'Moss's cottage' in the Appleton road, Miriam Harris holds her niece Hazel Bateman, while Clara Harris holds Miriam's daughter Jean.

The garden at 'Hurstcote', inspired by Leslie Brooke's children's books and managed by Arthur Boyles.

Vegetable gardening at Valley Farm, Farmoor, in 1940. Left to right: Ernest J. Webb, Ernest Barnett, Ted Rodgers. 'Digging for Victory'.

Some of the assembled parishioners who took part in the Victory Parade in 1945. (Photo: Edmonds)

Celebrating V.J. Day and 'Welcome Home'. Dinner being served outside the village hall. (Photo: Edmonds)

Celebrating the Festival of Britain in 1951 – folk dancing under the Lion Tree at the top of Leys Road. (Photo: Edmonds)

A float in the Festival of Britain procession. Mr Cox on left, Mrs Hutt, Bill Webb (in bowler), Harry Mitchell of Filchampstead on right (in topper); Mrs Drewett, back left, and Charles Costar. (Photo: Edmonds)

Cumnor Women's Institute celebrating its 40th anniversary in 1964. Left to right: Mrs Denton Brown, treasurer; Mrs Moss, president; Martha Franklin; Mrs Amy Belcher, vice-president; Mrs Mary Webb, founder member.

The 'summer outing', whether for the church choir, Sunday school, or village group, was a traditional feature of village life.

The Boys Brigade on church parade in 1953. On the left was Henry Thomas of Leys House, who served as Lord Lieutenant of Berkshire.

'In the bleak midwinter'. The High Street in 1947. (Photo: Edmonds)

In Chawley Lane in the early 1950s. Probably the last working horses in Cumnor. (Photo: Iris Wastie)

By 1932 the list of 'residents' for Cumnor in Kelly's Directory was lengthening. Only a selection is included below. 'Residents' tended to be householders of larger, freehold properties – the old term 'gentry' had been dropped. The commercial list was showing a growing range of non-agricultural businesses.

1932 KELLY'S DIRECTORY

CUMNOR RESIDENTIAL inc.
Abingdon Gwendoline Countess of, Oaken Holt
Bennett Frederick J.P., Norman Hurst
Brooke L.Leslie, Hurstcote
Brown Denton, School house
Douglas Stanley, Le Chateau, Hids Copse
Frewin Percy, The Brow, Cumnor hill
Griffiths Alfred, Rocklands, Cumnor hill
Hale John, Croft ho.
Hall Rev. Hy., M.A., (vicar)
Hinkins Chas., High Winds, Cumnor Rise
James Miss, Cutt's End
Jervois Miss, Cumnor Place
Lisemore Miss, Field house
Mortimore Fred, Sand Hill, Cumnor hill
Mott William, Kenilworth
Thackeray Miss, Larkbeare, Cumnor hill
Thomas Herbert, Long Leys house
Warland Cecil, Hillcrest
Webb Henry C., Church house

COMMERCIAL
Abery Wilfred J., farmer, Red House fm
Adams John, county police sergeant
Allington & Son, wheelwrights,Cumnor hl
Buckingham George, farmer, Pond farm
Busby Edward, clerk to Parish Council
Chawley Timber,Brick & Tile Works Ltd
Clanfield Charles, dairy farmer, Cutts end
Couling Joseph, dairyman, Lionsend
Cumnor Mens Social Club
Didcock Francis Geo., sen. shopkeeper
Franklin Boycott Wm., motor garage, Eynsham rd
Franklin Mrs, farmer, Swinford
Gee Jn, farmer, Denman's farm
Hale Jn., builder, Croft ho.
Hastings Harry, Vine P.H.
Haynes Hy., farmer, New farm
Hicks A. (Miss), confectioner
Hicks Geo., motor engnr, The Garage
Holiday Caravan Co. Ltd, caravan mkrs, Eynsham rd
Holifield Edmund & Son, plumbers etc
Howse Stephen, farmer, Lower Whitley
May Frederick, farmer, Bradley farm
Mortimer Frederick, mkt gardener, The Firs, Cumnor hill
Mygdal Carl, farmer, Farmoor
National Association for the Welfare of the Feeble Minded, Cumnor rise
Neale Wm., Bear & Ragged Staff P.H.
Nixey Wm., farmer, Busby's farm,Dean ct
Sheppard Geo., newsagent, Farmoor
Sheppard Wm., shopkeeper, Farmoor
Smith John, carpenter
Snell H., parish clerk
Tanner Raphael, farmer, Farmoor
Tyrrell Frank, farmer, Manor farm
Walker Percy, farmer, Rockley Field fm
Wastie Arthur, farmer, The Leys
Webb George, farmer, Burnt House farm
Webb Harry, farmer, Westfield farm
Wing Joseph, tobacconist & Post Office

SECTION THIRTEEN

Farmoor

Farmoor was originally the 'far moor', a belt of common meadow adjoining the larger Cumnor Meadow. The name became associated with a small group of local farmsteads in the 16th century. Beyond the meadows ran the Thames.

1870: the old flash weir and nearby alehouse ('The Fish'), managed by Joe Skinner. Henry Taunt considered it 'one of those picturesque places that artists love'.

In 1880 the old weir collapsed. The Thames Conservancy commission built a bridge there, but the house and alehouse were abandoned. A wooden bungalow was provided for a lock-keeper at nearby Pinkhill Lock.

Harry Smith, who succeeded Charles Sirett as lock-keeper, at Pinkhill in 1929. He was a keen gardener and won many prizes for his displays.

Harry Smith outside the new house, built in 1932. When a summer work camp for unemployed Welsh miners was held on the nearby meadows in 1935, musical evenings were held here and the lock decorated with fairy lights. 'The singing was beautiful – they had lovely voices', a resident recalls.

Haymakers on the meadow c.1914. The aeroplane was probably the first to land there. In the 1930s, Amy Johnson was among the aviators who enjoyed gliding at Farmoor – until the first line of pylons was erected.

In the 1930s parts of the meadow were exploited for gravel. The photograph shows Fred Curtis and Frank Bruton, employees of Curtis and Sons, extracting gravel. Hubert Curtis, a director of the firm, built a contemporary, white house on the hill top overlooking the meadows in 1934. 'I spent hours watching the herons on the meadows', Mrs Curtis said, 'and the pee-wits – you never hear them now.'

The meadow area was always liable to flooding. Filchampstead was a small settlement, 'filched' from the meadows' edge. Around 1700 it acquired the name of a popular dance, 'Tumble Down Dick'. There was an alehouse here. Photo c.1930.

Oaken Holt at the turn of the century.

Sir William Wilson Hunter.

The premises in 1993.

The first large house to be built in the area was Oaken Holt in 1891. Sir William Wilson Hunter bought land at Wood End from Lord Abingdon. Hunter, a friend of Kipling, had been a colonial official in India. He was an historian of India. His country house was named after a property his father had sought to buy in Wales. The first water supply came from a spring in Bean Wood. In his retirement here, Hunter played an active part in parish affairs.

During the Second World War, Oaken Holt was taken over for the headquarters of Westminster Bank and later became its training centre. After some years as a Buddhist Centre, it was purchased and adapted as a residential home. Its surroundings will be familiar to T.V. fans of 'Waiting for God'.

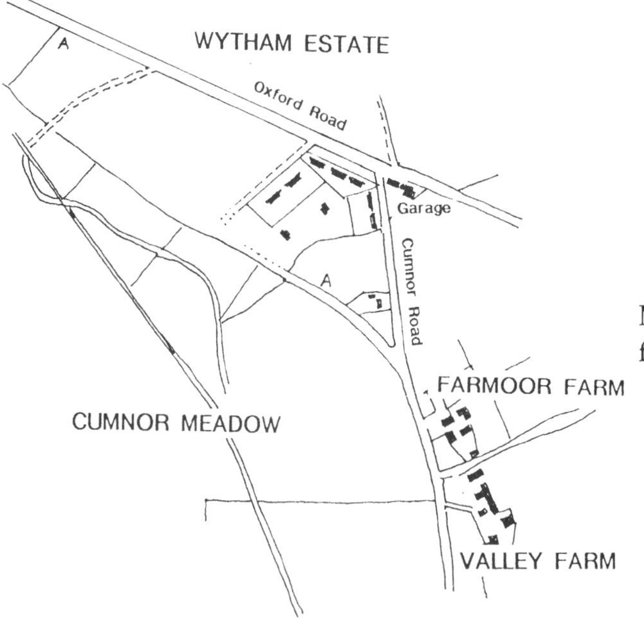

Map of Farmoor and the farm lands in 1922.

Farmoor Farm c.1925.

In 1922 Boycott Franklin, whose father farmed at Swinford, bought the freehold of Farmoor Farm from Lord Abingdon. The land was poor and farming generally was in recession. Two years later he bought nine ex-Army huts and erected them in the corner field by the Oxford Road. He rented them out. Betty Thornett, who took one of the first huts with her husband Christopher, remembers it as 'like a long camping holiday'. In 1927 Franklin sold land for building and the first bungalows were built (at sites marked 'A' on the map). Frances Wren recalls that her husband Fred had to sell his motorbike to pay the £50 deposit on their bungalow.

Bill Sheppard and his wife ran a small shop in their hut.

The last remaining hut in 1962, used as a hall, before demolition. 'Never seen so many mice in my life', Charles Sirett remembers; he helped to demolish it. The community built a new hall on the site.

Boycott Franklin's chief interests lay in engineering. Early in 1927 he obtained permission to build a garage on the corner of Cumnor Road. The farm was leased. This photo shows Bill Sheppard, with the garage across the road. The sign read: 'Second hand cars and motor cycles, any make supplied. Wireless sets, parts and accessories. Overhauls of every description.'

View of the garage in 1950. The pumps sold Cleveland Discol.

Farmoor Garage is one of the few to have remained in business from the 1920s to the present day. Photo: 1990.

In 1930 a shop was built to meet the needs of the growing community. This picture was taken in 1956. Bill Fletcher was standing in the doorway, while children waited for the school bus to Cumnor.

In 1935 help came from a number of quarters to provide a church at Farmoor. Money was raised locally and in Oxford to provide a hut. Earlier that year outdoor services had been held in a field in association with the unemployed miners' work camp. At the first church service at St. Mary's, Farmoor, people brought in their garden produce and the rafters were hung with travellers' joy.

'Idle days in summertime'. Boating at Swinford at the beginning of the century.

Farmoor's soccer XI in 1952. Left to right, back row: Cyril Keen, Peter Busby, Harold Bishop, Ken Edwards, Bill Warner, Peter Steptoe. Front row: Ken Turner, Brian Couling, Peter Stockford, Tony Read, Nobby Clack.

In the early 1930s a waterworks was built at Swinford to provide more water for Oxford.

Far greater changes came in 1960 with the building of the first huge reservoir on the meadows at Farmoor. A second reservoir was added in 1974.

Farmoor reservoirs and treatment works serve an area from Banbury to Swindon. The capacity is over three thousand million gallons, and Thames Water provides facilities for sailing, trout fishing and bird-watching.

Oxford Road in 1990. Until the by-pass was built north of Oxford, this was designated the A40, the main road to Wales.

Part of Meadow Close in 1990.

Although Farmoor today is perceived by many passing travellers as a modern development, the nearby meadows were the site of seasonal settlement in the Iron Age and Roman periods. Until the early years of this century the rural community comprised only scattered farmsteads. Boycott Franklin's enterprise created a new community, in the 1920s, which slowly established its own ways. The population of Farmoor doubled however when the building of the second reservoir in 1974 allowed an opportunity for the field below Oxford Road to be developed as Meadow Close.

SECTION FOURTEEN

Hillend

Hillend Farm, formerly the site of three farms, was part of the Wytham estate purchased from Lord Abingdon by Raymond Ffennell in 1920. Ffennell had a keen interest in outdoor education for deprived city children, and when Oxford City declined his offer of a site near Beacon Hill, he established facilities for outdoor education at Hillend. He died in 1943, leaving the Wytham estate to Oxford University. Hillend however has continued to serve as an important centre for environmental education.

Children at school in Wytham Woods in the 1930s.

One of the original dormitory buildings at Hillend.

SECTION FIFTEEN

Swinford

A drawing of Swinford toll bridge in 1859 (S. Hall). Until the 4th Earl of Abingdon paid for its construction in 1769, the river crossing was made by ferry boat. Parliament allowed the Earl to take the tolls tax-free. Today, under private ownership, higher tolls contribute to the cost of repairing the damage caused by heavy traffic use.

The large farm nearby was occupied from 1840 until 1995 by members of the Franklin family. This view of the farm was painted by J. Austin in 1856.

Boycott and Martha Franklin celebrating an anniversary with friends at Swinford c.1972.

SECTION SIXTEEN

Appleton: an Introduction

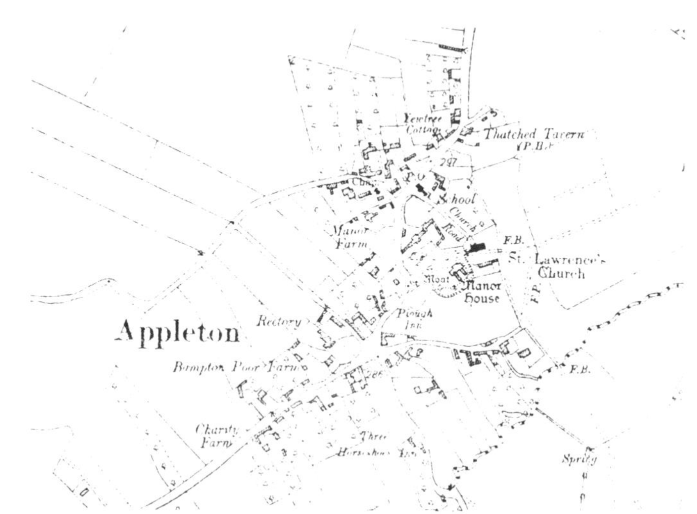

Appleton village in 1920.

Appleton village lies two miles south-west of Cumnor. In Roman times they were linked by a 'street', but the road between them today takes a more westerly line. Lying further from Oxford, the parish has suffered less than Cumnor from Oxford's suburban expansion. Appleton's population has doubled in this century – Cumnor's has increased five-fold. Appleton is first mentioned in a Saxon document referring to a tract of land called Earmundesleah, which included part of Besselsleigh. A Saxon boundary charter excluded Eaton, which was then part of Cumnor, but by 1086 Eaton was united with Appleton parish.

Appleton Manor House. (Photo: Oxford & County Newspapers 1987)

Appleton Manor

The main manor house in Appleton was built in the reign of Henry II, around 1190. Regarded by Pevsner as 'an amazing survival', it is probably the oldest of its kind remaining in England. The Fettiplace and Southby families were among its notable occupants. (Photo: T.Drury 1983)

The manor pond today, backed by the old barn which has been converted for residential use. (Photo: Hanson 1996)

There were in fact three manors in Appleton in medieval times but the other two have not survived. One was 'Tinteynes', which was moated and famous for its fine chimneys. Eaton was also a manor in its own right.

SECTION EIGHTEEN

St Laurence's Church

A view of St Laurence's parish church, Appleton, from the south-west. The south porch still houses a statue of the patron saint. Note the clock on the south wall of the tower. The picture was taken not long after the addition of the bell-lantern on the tower in 1861.

The church, little changed by the years, c.1935. The view is from the north-east and shows the new clock. (Photo: Leach)

The church interior in 1912, with its hanging candelabra, the Norman pillars and the old iron stove. (Photo: Taunt)

The Southby Chapel, also known as Lady Chapel. The pews to the left seated the occupants of the manor. The ledge near the hymn board held the charity loaves specially baked at the Hicks' family bakery.

Badgers' Well, beside the old lane down to the Thames, was first recorded in Saxon times. Later field names such as Holy Well Bottom bore testimony to its importance. The opening in the stone surround was 3 feet high. (Photo: Dix 1979)

SECTION NINETEEN

Bellringing

The name of Appleton has long been synonymous with the ringing and hanging of bells. Alfred White began a family bell foundry and bell-hanging business 200 years ago at the 'Greyhound' in Besselsleigh. A bellringing tradition at Appleton dates from 1818, when Robert Southby of Appleton Manor paid for replacing the three bells in the church tower with a ring of six. It is said he did this to appease villagers who had lost rights under his land enclosures. Alfred White added two further bells in 1854. In 1867 a newspaper advertisement appeared – a poem, which claimed, among other things:

> A. White & Sons Bellringers were made
> Because it was their fancy trade;
> In hanging bells they take delight
> To make them go with all their might.
>
> If you've a peal that's not quite right,
> Just drop a line to ALFRED WHITE,
> And with his SONS he will come down,
> Rehang the bells & make them sound.

Frederick White, 1834–1909, inherited his father's business at the 'Greyhound', Besselsleigh, where he was smith, bellhanger, wheelwright, clockmaker and publican. Around 1880 he moved to the 'Three Horseshoes' in Appleton and later moved to larger premises on the Eaton road where his descendants still carry on the business. It was Brian White who undertook the rehanging of the old bells and two new ones in Cumnor church tower in 1989.

Rev. F.E. Robinson. Living in Oxford, he became friendly with Frederick White, who taught him the art of bellringing. In 1859 he built the country house (now the School) at Besselsleigh but later moved to Appleton, where he was curate to the Rev. Butler. In 1861 he gave 2 bells to raise the ring to 10 bells; the church tower was already crowded and Alfred White solved the problem by adding a lantern to the tower. After Robinson became vicar at Drayton he would often walk the 8 miles to Appleton to ring the bells.

A record peal in 1921 led a parishioner to compose a song. It has been sung each year in commemoration of the event – in the 'Thatched Tavern'. It began:

Now you've called on me to sing you a song,
I'll sing you a song and it's not very long –
A song about ringing, I think it a treat
To sing when the Appleton ringers do meet.

Chorus: Hooray for the Appleton ringers I say
Who rang 10,000 on a November day.
Such ringing before you never did hear,
Ten thousand three forty of Caters Grandsire.

Stedman White rang the treble, he rang it so light;
George Holifield the second, he struck just right;
Harry Holifield the third, an old man was he
And when he finished he wanted his tea.

Thacker, the historian of the Thames at the turn of the century, heard from afar an 'ecstatic peal' from Appleton which 'tempestuously surged & died upon the wind as though from the moonlit spires of some forgotten city.'

The 'Thatched Tavern', in Eaton Road, in 1935. Here bellringers slaked their thirst. Who were all the children? Note the lane on the left. This was the line of the way to Cumnor from Roman times until the new road was built in 1829. (Photo: Leach)

On the corner of Badswell Lane in the Eaton road, Frederick White ran a blacksmith's and wheelwright's forge. This photograph, c.1900, shows Frederick White and, with the hammer, Chamberlain White. The old school can be seen across the road, in the background.

SECTION TWENTY

School

An Appleton school group from about 70 years ago. Left to right, back row: Mr Walter Hewitt, –, Gladys Cox, Mabel Cantwell, Bert Wakefield, Laura Taylor, Walter Clanfield, Fred Wells, Fred Purbrick. Middle: Cathleen Wells, Louise Robins, Mary Clanfield, Phyllis White, Kathleen Holifield, Tom Wakefield, Sydney Purbrick, Walter Purbrick, Nellie Cox, Ralph White, Bertram White, Nell White, teacher Evelyn Brown. Front: – Purbrick, Victor Wakefield, Nellie Purbrick, Gladys Taylor, –, William Wakefield.

'Children today', one senior citizen recalls, 'don't know what it's like to go to school taking a lunch of just a slice of bread and lard with sugar on.'

The school was founded in 1838 with one room, on land given by Robert Southby, but was enlarged in 1869. Rising numbers and modern needs led to the building in 1961 of a new primary school on adjoining land, which had once been orchard, given to the school as a playground by Mrs Katherine Timpson of Appleton Manor.

Eaton Road. Part of the old Church of England school can be seen on the right. Stallard's shop was to the left, and behind the white gates was a coalyard where one could buy a sack of coal, wheel it home on a sack truck, then dutifully bring the truck and empty sack back again. How times have changed! (Photo: Leach 1935)

The same scene today. The old school has gone and a new primary school built in the adjoining orchard down the lane.

SECTION TWENTY-ONE

Eaton Road

Stallard's shop and Post Office c.1935. 'This is where school children bought their sweets.' (Photo: Leach)

Outside one cottage in Eaton Road was the 'Pudding Tree' or 'Mushroom Tree'. It was in fact two trees, lovingly tended for many years by Mr. Louis Dymock. Clipping and shaping the dome was very difficult, especially the two peacocks which used to adorn it. This picture was taken before the last war. The tree has now gone.

The 'Plough' public house c.1935. The cottage beyond has now gone. Older villagers remember the Bung Club. Beyond George White's three storey house, the barns by his forge can be seen.

The 'Plough' in 1996.

SECTION TWENTY-TWO

The Centre of Appleton

The village centre in 1888. White's forge lay behind the white gates. The 'Plough' can be seen in the Eaton road, and beyond it the white gate in the manor wall which gave the rector a short cut from his rectory to the church.

A view c.1890 of the village centre and the start of the Eaton road.

Taunt's photograph in 1912 shows Hicks' shop and bakehouse. 'Sometimes in winter it was nice to lean against the bakehouse wall where the ovens had heated it.'

Hicks delivered bread around Appleton and also to Cumnor village, which had no bakery. Cumnor people sometimes had to wait for their bread as Hicks was fond of calling into the 'Vine' for a game of dominoes.

Today the war memorial occupies an honoured place on the village green.

SECTION TWENTY-THREE

The Three Horse Shoes

This picture from just before the Great War shows the 'Appleton Club' gathered outside the 'Three Horse Shoes' on its annual meeting day, held 'in peony time'. A march through the village with a band, and a church service, was followed by a Dinner at this public house. One participant remembered there was a separate 'gentlemen's table'. The Oddfellows society in Cumnor served a similar purpose in providing social welfare.

The 'Three Horse Shoes' in Oaksmere Road c.1935. Frederick White, who moved here from the 'Greyhound', had his workshops to the left of the public house. Among many other tasks he maintained the clock on Cumnor church tower.

SECTION TWENTY-FOUR

Badswell Lane

Badswell Lane in 1935. In those days it was known as 'The Sidelands', which seemed appropriate. The Congregational chapel is on the left. The white cottage was occupied by the Holifields. (Photo: Leach)

Cottages in Badswell Lane in 1935. Thanks to Preservation Orders they are still in being.

Badswell Lane in 1996.

SECTION TWENTY-FIVE

Netherton Road

Netherton Road, looking west, more than 60 years ago. Pond Farm lay to the right, Pound Farm to the left. The village pound was formerly nearby. The pond, with its stone bottom, can be seen to the right – it was used to swell the spokes of cart wheels in hot weather and to water the horses The poplar tree was lost in a severe gale about 20 years ago. (Photo: Leach)

A view from the same spot today. Pond Farm stands behind the high wall to the right.

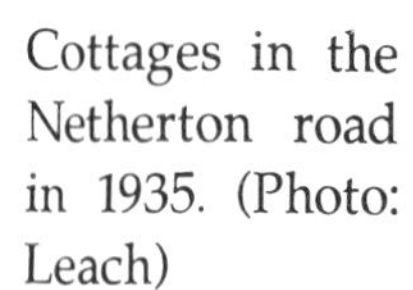
Cottages in the Netherton road in 1935. (Photo: Leach)

Houses a little further out of the village, built between the wars as the village began slowly to expand.

On the edge of the village in 1935, Tomkins' bungalow stood next to the house where the founder of Hill's Nurseries lived. The entrance to Millway Lane lay just beyond.

SECTION TWENTY-SIX

Eaton

Though part of Appleton parish from Norman times, Eaton was a manor in its own right and had a moated manor house. This, with the manorial lands, was purchased by Sir Thomas White, who founded St John's College in Oxford, and in 1555 he awarded Eaton to his college. Some of the manorial lands and properties lay in Cumnor.

A view in 1975 of the road running through Eaton. It reaches the Thames at Bablockhythe. (Photo: Oxford & County Newspapers)

The 'Eight Bells', photographed here in 1980, dates from the 16th century. The yew tree in front of it is said to be 100 years older. It was originally known as the 'Two Bells'. The old road ran to the rear of the building.

Pat and Derrick Johns, hosts at the 'Eight Bells' in 1988.

Ivor Fields, the Oxford photographer, prepares to take a picture of Eaton's assembled inhabitants in 1968. Many local people are recognisable in this interesting scene. (Photo: Oxford & County Newspapers)

SECTION TWENTY-SEVEN

Village Life

Early in the century, Mrs Moore, wife of the Rev. William Moore, stands apart from the gardener and two maids in the front garden of the rectory in Netherton Road. Did the distance reflect social attitudes of the time?

The bellringers of 1932. Left to right, back: R. Thomas Newman, F. Donald Boreham, George Holifield jun., Richard White, Fred White. Front: Walter Judge, Richard Post, Francis Taylor, George Holifield sen., William Simmonds, Cuthbert White.

Turn of the century in Eaton Road. Little remains of the farm in the background. The postman cycled from Abingdon to deliver and collect the mail and his route included Fyfield, Besselsleigh and Cumnor! No wonder his working day started at 4.30 a.m.

Celebrating the 60th anniversary of Appleton and District Women's Institute in 1986. Left to right: Myrtle Salmon, Mary Carter, Ann Biles, Maureen Alner, Christine Harris, Margaret Reading, Barbara Kinsey, Pam Wheeler.

Bill Painter and David Belcher laying, or 'plashing', a hedge in Ferry Lane, Eaton nearly 50 years ago. The craft is still practised and encouraged on one Eaton farm.

Frank White at his forge with Eddie Squires showing an expertise on the bellows. (Photo: Oxford & County Newspapers 1988)

The Rev. Paul Tuckwell, presented with a coffee set at Appleton School, where he had served as Chairman of Governors. With him were Mrs Tuckwell, and grandchildren Sarah and Trevor Griffiths. (Photo: Oxford & County Newspapers)

Sir Basil Blackwell, the well-known publisher and bookseller. An Appleton resident, he was photographed on the new bridge outside the church cottages in 1973. His house lay off the Netherton road. (Photo: Oxford & County Newspapers)

Mrs Cornish on the occasion of her 100th birthday. With her husband Howard she ran West Farm in Eaton for many years but also had links with Cumnor.

Howard Cornish farmed West Farm. He was also for many years a prominent member of Abingdon District Council.

Samuel Farrant and his wife ran Manor Farm in Eaton.

Appleton's hand-bell ringers in the early 1930s, outside the 'Thatched Tavern'. Left to right: Fred Steadman White, John White (who served in the London Metropolitan Police), Richard White, Fred White, Harry White and Cuthbert White.

1935 KELLY'S DIRECTORY

APPLETON

PRIVATE RESIDENTS

Blackwell Basil H., 'Ossa Field'
Gore Charles Henry O.B.E., M.A., Appleton House
Rowell Maj. Rouse, 'The Poplars'
Scanlan Rev.Gerald E.B., B.A., Rectory
Timpson Mrs Lawrence, The Manor House

COMMERCIAL

Brown Ralph, Thatched Tavern
Cooper Frederick, Plough P.H.
Cornish Howard, farmer, Manor farm
Cullen Albert, insurance agent
Dymock Edward, jobbing gardener
Edgington Thos., farmer, Pond farm
Eynstone Fanny (Mrs.), smallholder
Hicks Brothers, grocers
Holifield George & Sons, plumbers, glaziers & painters
Seeley Joseph, market gardener
Stallard Alice (Mrs.), shopkpr, Post office
Stephens Saml., Three Horse Shoes P.H.
Walford A.F. & Sons, farmers, Lower farm
Watkins Regnld S.G., timber merchant
White George & Sone, agricultural engnrs
White Arthur, farmer, Field farm
White Cuthbert G., undertaker & Parish Clerk.
White Richard, church bell hanger

EATON

COMMERCIAL

Cooper Wm.Hy., Manor farm
Cornish Howard, farmer, West farm
Faulkner Chas., beer retailer